# BASEBALL...

## IT'S NOT JUST A GAME

# BASEBALL...
## IT'S NOT JUST A GAME

My **36 Years** in Little League Baseball

By Coach Bobby Nicholds

Order this book online at www.trafford.com
or email orders@trafford.com

Most Trafford titles are also available at major online book retailers.

Printed in the United States of America.

ISBN: 978-1-4269-5555-6 (sc)
ISBN: 978-1-4269-5556-3 (hc)
ISBN: 978-1-4269-5557-0 (e)

Library of Congress Control Number: 2011900563

*Trafford rev. 01/20/2011*

 www.trafford.com

North America & International
toll-free: 1 888 232 4444 (USA & Canada)
phone: 250 383 6864 ♦ fax: 812 355 4082

**T**his Work is dedicated
to my friends and heroes

Kimberly Ann Shroyer

Buddy Jones

Harold Loftin

Reggie Frye


And to my son,

Robert Nicholds

Sarah Bennet & Coach Bobby
Sarah & her family are my special friends.

# CONTENTS

# A LITTLE BIT OF MY HISTORY...
## with baseball

It all started when I was a child growing up in Glendale, Texas which is a small community about 25 miles northeast of Huntsville, Texas. Glendale is located between the towns of Trinity and Groveton in Trinity County. This is deep east Texas for all of you with a map out. Ok, Ok...just kidding ... but you get the idea.

I was the only child of Cleo and Jane Nicholds. They were the greatest parents a boy could have growing up in a small community in Texas. I found out early what having loving, caring, and joyful parents can mean to a child.

We lived next door to the Glendale Baptist church and I still own the old home place there. God used me when I was a 6 year old boy. I would go to the little Methodist church also in Glendale. At that time, my parents did not go to church but as a young boy I always had a desire to know about Jesus. Finally, one day God used me to reach my parents and the Lord saved them and my father became a Baptist preacher.

My father, Cleo Nicholds really had no education but it proved to me that God can use anyone who is willing to let him. God is not looking for someone's ability but their availability.

So, I guess you're wondering where baseball comes in for who I am in life. As I said, I loved baseball and since I had no brothers or sisters I would play baseball by myself. Have any of you ever played baseball by yourself? It's not easy to do…BUT…in Glendale we had a field behind the old home place…SO…I made myself a baseball field. I would take a baseball bat, gather up some rocks and hit rocks as if I were hitting baseballs in a real game. I also would try to find a place where I could catch a rubber ball or tennis ball using a back porch step or wall for the rebound. It works if you like playing catch with yourself.

Then around 1954, we moved to Henderson, a town also in east Texas, because my father went to work for an oil company in Longview, Texas which was a few miles up the road. We lived in Henderson for a while and then moved about 5 miles out in the country.

As you might guess, again I made myself a baseball field. I can still remember throwing a rubber or tennis ball up against the chimney of the house, then I would hit the ball, drop the bat, catch the ball and throw it up against the chimney as if I was throwing the runner out. I had a friend who lived in Henderson in a subdivision and there were a few boys who lived in that subdivision and there was a field there where they had made a baseball field. In the summer, I would get on my bicycle with my glove, bat, and ball and ride to Henderson which was around 4 miles and play baseball all day and get home before dark.

Back in the middle fifties, we didn't have video games or computers to keep us in the house so we played outside. I still say being outside is healthier for you and you meet more people. Plus you all know baseball is better for you because it is a physical sport. I also believe that we would have healthier children today if we could see some boys and girls playing sand lot baseball.

We lived in Henderson from 5th grade until the summer before my freshman year in high school. Then my father was laid off from his job in Longview, so we moved back to Glendale and I enrolled in Groveton high school for my freshman year.

Since we lived 12 miles from Groveton, I could not play high school baseball because I had no way home after practice every day but I got to play high school baseball my junior year because there was a boy in Glendale who had a car, so now, I had a way home after practice.

For the record, in case you were wondering, I became the starting 2nd baseman my junior year in high school and the starting shortstop my senior year. However, I still am a 2nd baseman in my heart. I just wanted you to know a little bit about me before I start to tell you the rest of my story.

I graduated from high school in 1963 and decided to attend East Texas Barber College in Tyler which is a town in northeast Texas about 30 miles west of Longview in Smith County. I completed my training, received my state license and became a barber. After a short stint as a barber for a friend of mine in Lufkin, which is a town 70 miles southeast of Tyler, I decided to move to Trinity and opened up my own barbershop but had slow business because there was already another barber shop in town. Sooooo...I went to work in a barber shop in Huntsville for a good friend of mine who was a great boss. However, this was the time when my journey was about to begin into Little League baseball.

## MY ADVENTURE BEGINS...

My mother told me one time that if I worked as hard at my school work as I did playing baseball and studying major league baseball players and their batting averages I could be anything I wanted to become in life. I think she was right and since I was in Huntsville at this time in my life, I knew that I wanted to work with kids soooooo...I wanted to see if I could get a Little League baseball team that might need a Coach.

Well, here I am a young man just starting out with all these veteran coaches in the Huntsville, Texas Little League…oooooboy.

So, we had the tryouts at the little league field in Huntsville and we watched all the players try out for all the different teams. After everyone was through with tryouts, we told them they could go home and we would call them and let them know which team they would be on.

I realized I was the really new kid on the block when I was walking across the street with all these veteran coaches to a restaurant so we could all sit down and draft our players. I was so nervous but I was excited because I was about to start my career coaching Little League baseball. They had a Pee Wee team that needed a coach.

Soooooo…they gave THAT team to me.

# THE LUMBERJACKS... my 1st team

The team was the Lumberjacks. They were my first team and all teams had sponsors. My team's sponsor was a building supply and they were great to us. They would give us whatever we needed...bats, balls and uniforms. In fact, one summer, I and some of the other coaches in the Pee Wee league took the whole league to the Astrodome for a baseball game. Our team sponsor gave me a check for the tickets and spending money for my players. I felt real close to my team and their parents. I tried to teach my ballplayers that baseball was more than just a game. We would have prayer before each game. By the way, we need more of THAT, don't you think?

I always tried to teach my players the value of working together for a purpose and being there for each other and building friendships that could last a lifetime.

Sometimes I get my baseball picture album out and look at the team pictures and it still brings back memories of the kids I managed as Coach of the "Lumberjacks" for 12 years and to this day I still feel proud of my first team.

Coach Bobby Nicholds First T-Ball
Team in Trinity -Spring of 1980
This was the beginning of T-Ball in Trinity

## WHEN I GOT TO TRINITY...

When I got to Trinity, I still had a desire to coach baseball and work with kids. However, there was not a team open because the Little League coaches had been there for years. I noticed Trinity didn't have a T-Ball League...sooooo I decided to start one in town.

I will never forget that we found a large vacant lot in town and the owners of that lot let us build a baseball field on it. We had 3 boys' teams and 2 girls' teams. My boys' team was the Dodgers and we also had the Reds and the Tigers. The 2 girls' teams were the Angels and the Bluebirds.

We had a great year and NOW in Trinity, we have a T-Ball League, Machine Pitch League, Little League teams and also a Pony League. The next summer, we had more boys who came out for Little League so they formed 2 new Little League teams, the Dodgers and the Red Devils. Well, I took the Dodgers and my friend Gene took the Red Devils. Later, we changed the team from Red Devils to the Cardinals.

Back when I was coaching my T-Ball (Dodgers), I will never forget a kid I picked in the 1st round. That kid was Chris and he was one of the best players in the League if not the best one overall. However, before the season started that year, Chris got sick and ended up in the hospital. I, of course, went to see Chris to see how he was feeling.

I met his mother in the hospital

room and she told me even though he was sick, all Chris could think or talk about was being my 2nd baseman for the Dodgers. So, I told him there was no need for him to worry...he was my 2nd baseman and all he needed to do was get well. Chris did get well and it was to be a great season and a small victory had

just played out in Chris' life and mine.

## KIDS LOVE TO PLAY BALL... SO

There are times when I look back and recall what it was like before video games. Do you remember those days? Yeah, I thought that might take you back to a simpler time when everyone usually ended up outside the house looking for something to do or play or both after school.

In the Trinity Little League, we let every boy and girl play baseball. If their parents didn't have the money to sign them up in the league, we let them play anyway. It was an easy and right decision.

As our league started growing, I went to the city fathers to see if they would help us build bigger. So, the City of Trinity decided they would help us build two more baseball fields next to our 2 existing baseball fields because we had enough land to get it done. Where there's a will, there definitely can be a way. Let me explain about the scenario. The city had bought all of the fence that we needed for the project but we needed someone to put it together. Sooooooo, I decided to ask the Texas Department of Corrections (the Texas prison system) if they would furnish some inmates to help us with the fence construction for the 2 fields. The TDC brought us 10 inmates. All we had to do was feed them all a noon meal. So for the price of hamburgers, fries and Coca-Colas for a couple of days, those inmates did beautiful construction work and those baseball fields are still standing tall and strong for the kids today. Sometimes, I think that it's moments in time like that which are the most special.

## THINGS CAN HAPPEN...

Sometime later just to walk onto that baseball field and look around to see the green grass and the base lines after you have worked all day on that field made me feel like I had done something good to help our players have a place they could be proud of and look good. When I looked it over, I felt happy in my soul.

One year we got to host the District Tournament in Trinity and I was so excited about other teams coming into our town to play in our tournament. I got some of the coaches together and we started working on the fields to get them ready. We worked hard for about 2 weeks and we had the fields looking gooood.... and we had a great tournament that year. It's always amazing to me how much people can accomplish when we pull together.

If you have ever coached or umpired or have been involved
in Little League baseball then you have a lot of memories as I do. Some

of my moments in Little League ball were unforgettable, with explosive strangeness, and all kind of things that can happen in a Little League baseball game. Here come some recollections that I want to share with you. I hope you enjoy them. They're true. I promise.

# YEAH, THESE THINGS REALLY HAPPENED....

One of my greatest memories in Little League baseball happened when I was still coaching in Huntsville. We were in the championship game and as always I played all my players on my team. The best hitter in the league came up with 2 men on base. We were 1 run ahead and there were 2 outs. I was in the dugout and at this point quietly praying, "Lord, please don't let him hit the ball to the outfield" because I had just put my subs in the outfield.

The ugly truth was I had a centerfielder that couldn't catch a cold much less a baseball at all...BUT...

This time, when the best hitter in the league did hit the ball to the outfield, he managed to hit my centerfielder's glove with the ball while he was running toward it and he DID catch it. A little hero was born that night and my "Lumberjacks" were champions. Plus we carried the "little hero" off the field on our shoulders. That catch seemed to instill in that young man so much confidence in himself. I have always told my players that you can be anything in life that you want to be as long as you believe, work and let God lead you.

## SIDE NOTES...

I wanted to tell you also about the time we were in the middle of a game when I looked out in left field. There was my left fielder, his glove on the ground, with a hot dog in his right hand and a coke in his left. Soooo, I had to call a time out and his father and I had to go and remind "hungry" boy of some basic rules.

There was another game where one of my players hit a ground ball and started running to first base. Instead of going to second base…he just kept running down the first base foul line. I guess we all can get overly excited sometimes.

## SIDE NOTES II...

Then there was the time a boy on the other team was running to second base but right before he got there, my second baseman got between him and the bag and would not let him get to the base and they went round and round.

Believe me when I say a lot of fans enjoyed what they saw that game. When you can get joy and laughter like that at the ballpark...you can forget about your problems and just enjoy life for a while.

# SOMETIMES YOU WONDER...

There are times though when you wonder about people. This was one of those times. It was when I was still coaching in Huntsville. We were in a game; there were 2 outs and the bases were loaded and the best hitter in the league came to bat. Well, he hit a ground ball to my shortstop who threw the ball home to force the runner out at home which ended the inning. Then we came to bat and they got us out.

Lo and behold, the boy who had just batted came up to bat again the next inning, so I called time out and went up to the plate umpire and told him that this boy had just batted the last inning. The umpire said he didn't remember so he went over to talk to the official scorer who said she did not know how to write a force out on the scorebook so they let the boy bat again. He hit a home run and beat us.

After the game, their coach came up to me and said he didn't know that boy had just batted. If you think I believed that story, you are wrong; he knew that he had just batted because that boy was the best hitter in the league. The problem is that coach showed he was out there for the wrong reason and that he wanted to win no matter who it hurt. All the players and fans knew what he had done. Bad sportsmanship.

# SOMETHING'S MISSING...

There was a coach in Trinity who was an older man and he had a good team; a team that should have won the league championship but here is where teamwork comes in. Even with all the good players he had on his team, the most important thing was missing and that was teamwork. He had the best players in the league but they played as individuals and not as a team. They didn't understand that to win they had to play as a team.

You know that is like life itself, we all have to work together to achieve what is good for all. When we do that we can really make a difference in our lives.

Little League is not only teaching children to play baseball but it is also teaching them about building relationships with their teammates and also all the other players in the league. So someday when little league is over they will have built some friendships along the way.

One day one of my players came to see me and I was so happy to see him and to find out what a fine young man he had become and that he had a successful business. That is the joy I get out of working with kids.  When you really help someone and you see that they turned out alright then that is all the reward I need.

## BUT THERE WAS THIS ONE TIME...

I thought I would also tell you this story because…well, it was like this. I was coaching in Huntsville in the early days and I had to have ear surgery one day. So when I got out of the hospital they gave some pills that made me really relax. When I took one of those pills, I really didn't much care what was happening or had happened. Anyway, it was game day and I went driving up to the game with my head wrapped up like a mummy. We started the game and really got beat badly but I remember it as a happy type day…know what I mean?

## DAVID…(good kid)

The boy was named David. The first time I saw him practice, I told all the other coaches that David would play pro ball someday. All of you who are coaches know the David type. This kid was a tall, blond prototype ballplayer. Do you know what I mean?

Well, David did play for 10 years in the minor leagues but did have to have several surgeries on his arm. However, he did have a great attitude and definitely was my kind of player.

A year or so back, I got to see David for the first time in years at an event. David made me feel really good when I heard him say "there's my coach!"

We got to talking about all his experiences and it was great to get back together after all these years. I was so proud of David and the man he turned out to be plus he was a successful businessman. David really was the type of player every coach dreams about because he was just "coachable"...he did what you asked him to do and much more. I always hoped that in some way that I helped David and I had some positive influence in his life. Now, David is coaching his son in sports and he told me, that he didn't realize that there was so much involved in coaching. The life experiences for all us who've coached just keeps going on.

## SIDE NOTES III...

There were a couple of semi-strange things that happened that I wanted to tell you about while they were on my mind.

One day, I was standing outside of my barber shop in Trinity and a car went by; the young man in the car shouted "Hi Coach!"

"I bet you don't remember me!" It was one of my favorite players from the past. So I said "Hi George! Happy

Birthday!" He had such a puzzled look. I didn't tell him I had seen a happy birthday wish for him on a bank sign in Huntsville the day before he saw me.

Then there was a time one day when we having a practice and my shortstop would not get down on the ground balls that were being hit to him.

When I finally stopped everything; I turned to Arthur and said "What's the matter with you?...Get down and get the ball!"

He said, "Coach, I can't …I got arthritis!" Arthur was 8 years old at the time.

OR…there was this time very recently when I was at a friend of mine's feed store and there was this big guy inside who said "Hi Coach!" to me. At first I didn't recognize him, then he told me his name was Brandon and I remembered him as one of my best ballplayers from SOME time ago. He lives in Dallas and the company he works for pays him to play in tournaments on the weekends. Nice work if you can get it…makes a coach proud to be around the game.

## SPEAKING OF BEING PROUD...

I'm so proud of the 2007 High School baseball team here in Trinity. Our Trinity Tigers won the semi-regional championship. They got within one game playing for the state championship. These same boys grew up in the Trinity Little League program.

As they went through the Little League program, we tried to teach them baseball but also about teamwork and when they went out of town; how to conduct themselves. The Trinity Tigers were successful in the 2007 baseball season because of the foundation that was laid out for them. There is so much involved in developing our young people if we would just stop and think about it.

# KIDS WILL AMAZE YOU...

I remember this one game we were playing and one of my best players was on 3rd base with my big slugger up to bat. My slugger hits this line shot down 3rd base line that hits my player standing on third base and knocks him down but he gets up and heads for home plate and scores because there just wasn't any "quit" in this kid.

Sometimes, you just wonder why kids do what they do and for what possible reason.  So to make a long story longer, some time later we had the county fair going on in town and this same kid I was telling you about (whose name is Scott) decided to play at the "greasy" pole exhibit at the fair.

When Scott got through having fun climbing the "greasy" pole exhibit he realized he had no skin on the top of his feet and his hands were messed up too. He asked for my help so I helped him put cream on his hands and feet. Then I taped him up because he told me that he was going to play in the ball game that night and he did play. However, that's the kind of kid Scott was for the team.

## MORE ABOUT SCOTT...

There was this one game when Scott got really upset with his teammates, which I couldn't blame him, because they would not put out their best effort. So, he went home and told his mother that he just couldn't take their attitude anymore. He told her he gave a 100% effort and they didn't care if they won or lost.

Scott's mother called me and said she wanted me to talk with him. So I went over there and told him that I needed him and not to worry about the other players as long as you gave it your best that is all you can do.

Today, I am so proud of Scott and every time he's in town I try to see him. He is a good example of being all you can be. He's let nothing stop him from being successful. I just hope that being Scott's little league coach had a little influence on his being a great young man.

When he reads this book he will know it's him that I was so proud of and to be honest, his brother is my best friend.

# THE MAN IN BLUE. ... REALLY?

Then after coaching for years, I became President of the Trinity Little League and that was an experience in itself. I also started umpiring, you know, the Man in Blue. There were many fans who would say, "Blue, put your glasses on!" or "Blue, you're missing a good game!"

Normally the fans that caused me the most trouble knew little about baseball. Do you know what I mean? Anyone?

Being human though…there were times when I would have to stop the game and talk to
some of the fans about their attitude.

One time we lived about 3 blocks from the baseball field and after work I would go home and get my umpire uniform on and walk to the field. One day while walking to the field, I came across 6 players from another team and they were sitting on the sidewalk waiting for something or someone in order to go somewhere.

ANYWAY, I spoke to them as I passed by and I started to hear things fall behind me and as I looked back, these same players I had just passed were throwing rocks at me.

You know, it just wasn't easy being the Man in Blue even when you're off duty. While I was umpiring, there were coaches who would tell some of their players, you know, the ones who could not hit the ball just to stand there hoping they would get a walk. You know, we can also apply that situation to life.  If you don't try things, you will never get to first base.

But, I do remember one particularly amazing thing. When I was umpiring, it was always interesting to me how coaches on the teams could see the pitches better than me when I was looking over the left shoulder of the catcher. Yeah, I know...

# MAN IN BLUE II...

While I was umpiring, I will never forget one of my friends used to ride me about my umpiring to just have fun with me. Well, one night before a game that his team was playing; I was lining the field and I went over to the dugout with the lining machine and I made a small box and told him to stay in that box during the game. This was mainly because he would get so excited in the game that he would jump around like a frog.

That same coach cost me an umpire one year. I had a base umpire quit because this coach stayed on him so bad he couldn't take it anymore. I mean…COME ON PEOPLE!

Then there was this coach with his video camera. Nooo, wait…I can't say what I really want to say. However, this coach videotaped every game so he could show me every pitch I called incorrectly. God forgive me but I was hoping that a foul ball would take out that video camera…permanently.

## BE ON YOUR TOES...

Just a couple thoughts here; because when you're umpiring a Little League baseball game you have to be on your toes because you don't know what is going to happen next.

When I was umpiring, you had to be careful because some pitchers were pretty wild so I would always stand behind the catcher. Plus there was always a catcher who would jump up and throw his face mask in the air and it would come down on top of the umpire. I still hate those kinds of "surprises."

While I'm thinking about it, I want to mention about 3 little ladies that were seemingly always at the game supporting the kids and the "Man in Blue." They were such fans that we bought them caps and shirts that said "Number 1 Fan"…it was a special time that made us smile.

## KIDS AND SUPPORT GO TOGETHER...

At this point, there are still a couple of things that I need to mention because they have had importance in kids' lives.

During my years of coaching, I had some boys who played on my teams whose parents I never met for whatever reason. These kids became special to me because they needed a friend to talk to about things like how school was going and to sit with them when their parent was an hour late picking them up after practice. It has always been important to LISTEN to the kids. I know most all of you would agree with me.

# REMEMBER TO PLAY WITH STYLE...

As I watch the Little League World Series each year, I see great examples of sportsmanship from all the teams. You see players displaying great sportsmanship in many ways; like a batter being hit by a pitch and the pitcher going over to see if he is ok. When a player hits a home run, I've seen players on the other team congratulate him...we always need more of that type play.

Also during the Series, they put microphones on the coaches so that people watching the game can hear what they were saying to their players. When talking to their players, all these coaches would always build the kids up by telling a boy if he made an error to just shake it off and it was ok or if he had to take a pitcher out of the game, he would tell that pitcher he did a good job. I think the best thing these coaches did, and they did this almost every time, was before they went back to the dugout they would tell these kids to have fun. I applaud these coaches for wanting the kids to have fun AND a championship style of play. To me, THAT is what the definition of "style" is all about for baseballers.

For all of us 'round here the prime example of "style" is the Dixie Youth League National Baseball organization and Trinity's been a member for a long, long time.

## MY FRIENDS AND HEROES...

As you go through life, we all have people who drop in and out of our lives and affect who we are and what we accomplish in life. I think we've all had the family members, the next door neighbor, the uncle, the co-worker or others that we miss for the difference that their presence made in our lives.

After 36 years in Little League, there are 4 of them I wanted to tell you about here. They are all gone now but all 4 will always be in my heart. Because I knew these 4 people, I was a better coach, better friend and I think I was a better man.

# KIMBERLY ANN SHROYER...

There were several things that always jumped out when you met Kim. She was such an upbeat and supportive person, you just felt good to be around her. It seemed like her dark hair and greenish eyes were everywhere.

She absolutely was a perfect Little League mother. She was the fundraiser and she loved the kids. She was a mother. Kim had 2 boys and a girl of her own. She never lost her zeal for what we were trying to get accomplished. She represented us well.

She was the "team mother". She left this planet way too early considering how much we all needed her. I'm sure you all have your own "Kim" who will do whatever it takes because they love the kids and the game.

Our Kim was exactly that way. We could not have done what we did if she had not been in our life. She left this planet way too soon for us but heaven gained a bright angel with a great smile. We miss our Kim even today.

# Kimberly Ann Shroyer

## BUDDY JONES...

How can I accurately describe Buddy Jones for you? He was about 5'8", stocky build with wavy black hair. He was retired from the Texas Department of Corrections. He loved working with the kids, respected the game and was always learning the game and asking questions. Buddy was my assistant coach and was always supportive of me and the kids. He was a good friend and always had a neat appearance. He never drank alcohol or smoked cigarettes. There was a time though when he was in a place called Vietnam and being sprayed with a thing called Agent Orange that would shorten his life. Buddy was another one that we certainly could not have accomplished what we did without him. Buddy was a true champion. I know that everyone still misses him. I would bet that a lot of you have your own "Buddy" or more than one would be probably more like it. Am I right or what?

Buddy Jones with our Dodger Team.
Buddy was always my right hand man.
I miss you so much, friend.

# HAROLD LOFTIN...

The 3<sup>rd</sup> member of my friends and heroes was Harold Loftin. He was another retiree. He was retired from the Champion-Southland paper company. He enjoyed the game but was always learning baseball especially lineups and a lot of substitutions. He was about 5'9", skinny with a high energy nervousness that would have made Barney Fife look calm.

Like the others before him, Harold loved the kids and loved coaching.

We couldn't have done what we did without Harold being there. Some things were just a given. Do you know what I mean?

Harold Loftin and his Little League team,
the Braves. I called him Mr. Slim.

## REGGIE FRYE...

One night I was talking to a parent about my friend Reggie. It seems that one night Reggie was sitting on the tail gate of his truck next to this couple watching the ballgame. Their son was coming up to bat. Reggie, who did not know that this was their son, said it had to be this boy coming up to bat and he was going to get a hit and win the game and to the parents' delight, that's exactly what happened.

That was my friend Reggie. He always had something positive to say about the kids and just knew how to build them up. Reggie was the "grandfather" figure to a multitude of Little League kids during those years. Reggie was about 6'1 ", semi-balding and retired from Phillips Oil. He was our game announcer. He would always have something to say about my umpiring so everyone could hear it. It was all good natured fun and I still remember on those clear nights when the P.A. system was working well that Reggie's voice would carry for miles or so it seemed. Reggie always added color to the game. Reggie meant so much to the kids and all of us. It has always been true that it's not what you take from this world when you go, it's what and who you leave behind.

Reggie at his favorite place on game night
as he announced the baseball games and
tried to help Umpire Bobby call the games.

We lost Reggie some time back to cancer but before it was his time to go be with the Lord, we all were able to be with him one last time. It was a special period in time for all of us. One of our players named Ray got to officially present a plaque to Reggie that told him how much he meant to all of us because he was a true champion and we were honored to know him.

Reggie Frye at the Little League baseball
fields in Trinity, Texas

Sometimes, even with all the honors that people get, it's better just to hear a testimony from someone who you affected with their own words.

The following was from Patrick Ross.

# THE LEGACY OF REGGIE...

Now that I'm older, reflecting back, Reggie was a great asset to this community. The attention to detail and the dedication Reggie put towards Trinity's youth baseball was indicative of the type of person he was. Sadly, as is within most cases, you do not appreciate what someone has done until they are gone and no longer doing it.

I began playing baseball in Trinity in 1985 as a boy. I was a first year

T-ball player then, but Reggie's vigor for our youth baseball did not escape my attention even at a young age.

Reggie was the game announcer for the Little League in the middle baseball field, and anytime you went to the baseball complex you heard his voice ringing out over the intercom. What Reggie unknowingly did was create an almost electric atmosphere of excitement that spread through the entire sports complex. Crowds showed up to watch those games and you couldn't help but to be drawn to that Little League field.

I spent three years on the T-ball field waiting to make it to the big times on the Little League field. That was the atmosphere he had created.  When you were on that Little League field, it felt like you were in the big game, and it felt like a big game because Reggie called it.

I played Little League for 4 years on that field and I don't remember Reggie ever missing a game. What

Reggie was good at, OR really great at, was that he made every player feel special.

I know he made me feel special. I don't think I ever spoke to him in person but he still made me feel special. It was the things he would say while you were up to bat like, "Boy, you better watch out for this kid, he's got a good eye" or "This kid knows how to swing a bat, you'd better watch him." Even when you were on the field or running bases he'd make those little comments that in hindsight, really added so much to the Game. That is what made it the big times, those little comments like your record for the night in batting, or the mention of a good play you had made in the field.

I believe Reggie made every kid feel that way. He had something good to say about every player. Even if you didn't get to play very much, when you were on that field, Reggie called your name and number and remembered something about you. Reggie made those games mean something. You felt as if you were actually playing for something special. There seemed to be a larger turnout for players and spectators then as well. Reggie created a sense of a strong community on that baseball field, a sense of community that has somehow withered over the years.

As those years passed on, so did Reggie, and the ball field is a different place now. Twenty years later, I'm now at the baseball field and I'm watching my son play. There is no announcer shouting over the loudspeaker, the crowds do not seem to be into the game as much anymore, and the excitement is gone. When I go to the baseball field now, I can't help but remember how it was and I wish my son could experience that. I think that for those of us that were involved back then, we can truly appreciate the impact that Reggie had on us all: the players, coaches, spectators, umpires, organizers and the community. I want to thank him for that. Reggie, you are surely missed.

Sincerely,

Patrick Ross

# WE BUILT IT AND THEY DID COME....

It has been an amazing 36 years since I started my journey and for everyone who's been on this trip with me, I say thank you and God Bless You. For all the Kims, Buddys, Harolds, and Reggies out there, keep loving the kids; you are and have always been special for a special game.

# FINALLY...just one more thing

His name is Robert Nicholds and he's my son. Robert and his family live in Athens, Wisconsin. They have a beautiful home on 20 acres of land and Robert has his own trucking business. I am so proud of my son. He is blessed with a great family. He has a beautiful wife, a daughter and 2 sons.

You guessed it, I'm going to tell you about my grandkids. Bethany is his oldest and she is a beautiful young lady. I am so proud that my mother got to see and spend time with Bethany before my mother went to be with the Lord.

Then there is Lane…I don't know where to start about this boy. He's as tough as boot leather and all boy. He plays baseball and football. My son is always telling me about his football career because I don't get to see them much.

There is also Lance…who has been through some real serious health problems in his young life. He is still quite a character and he showed me one time by setting his grandpa straight on one or two things.

One summer, I met Robert and his family in Florida for a vacation. We had stopped to eat at this place were outside on a picnic table. A squirrel came up to me and I started feeding it.

Lance quickly told me, "Grandpa, didn't you see the sign?" The sign said "Don't Feed The Animals."

Tina is Robert's wife and I am so proud she is my daughter-in-law. Tina is a great mother and she teaches her children right from wrong. My son could not have picked a better wife. I want to thank Tina for taking care of my son.

Thank you and I love all of you.

# My son Robert Nicholds & Family
## Wife Tina
## Daughter Bethany
## Son Lane
## Son Lance

## ABOUT THE AUTHOR

Today, Coach Bobby Nicholds is Judge Bobby Nicholds, a Justice of the Peace in Trinity County in East Texas. I hope that you will enjoy all these stories as Coach Bobby reflects back on his 36 years of Little League Baseball, East Texas style.